FIRE IS NOT A COUNTRY

FIRE IS NOT A COUNTRY

poems

Cynthia Dewi Oka

TriQuarterly Books / Northwestern University Press
Evanston, Illinois

TriQuarterly Books
Northwestern University Press
www.nupress.northwestern.edu

Printed in the United States of America

10 9 8 7 6 5 4 3 2 1

Library of Congress Cataloging-in-Publication Data

Names: Oka, Cynthia Dewi, author.
Title: Fire is not a country : poems / Cynthia Dewi Oka.
Description: Evanston, Illinois : TriQuarterly Books/Northwestern University Press,
    2022.
Identifiers: LCCN 2021022695 | ISBN 9780810144217 (paperback) | ISBN
    9780810144224 (ebook)
Subjects: LCSH: Families—Poetry. | BISAC: POETRY / American / Asian American |
    POETRY / American / General | LCGFT: Poetry.
Classification: LCC PS3615.K33 F57 2022 | DDC 811.6—dc23
LC record available at https://lccn.loc.gov/2021022695

For my son

CONTENTS

FIRE IS NOT A COUNTRY

MEDITATION ON THE WORTH OF ANYTHING

A tall man wipes ashes from his lips. "I'll pay you,"

he says. "If you're worthy." From the lamp of his skull, a steeple
rises. Roaches seek warmth in the dead bells, while cherry

blossoms burst their green corsets. My mother at the end

of a 12-hour shift at the factory will heat rice-and-vegetable soup,
cooked last weekend and kept frozen to last her six working

days, to eat while watching reruns of *The Good Wife*.

She does not always understand what Julianna Margulies is
saying. Sometimes she weeps because memory is long and

bendy, a red line that curves around the globe instead of

cutting through the center. It begins on a piece of rock
represented on the globe by a bump under the fingertip. A body

at the bottom of a well. Which is a good place—if

someone's kid could lower a piece of mackerel down to you
in a pail, twice a day, cleaned of its bones. Strange how

expensive rice was then with so many bodies in

the river, puddles, trailing their red ribbons. When I told
my mother I was going to start organizing workers, she

slapped me with the same hand that used to soothe the long,

bumpy scar on my father's chest. I have to make time to cry, and
eat. Fuck that kamikaze shit. It was not just from grief that

shocks of hair fell from my head to the kitchen floor. I wore

four-sizes-too-big-but-ironed jeans for the better part of high
school and threatened kids by thumbing a knife across

the skin of an orange because my parents believed even

an ordinary man of no particular feat or achievement could
be brought back to life when God wanted to prove

a point. In other words, there could be a universal language

in whose syntax fire is not a country. Sometimes, it's like I'm almost
there. Some mornings, smoking, I lock eyes with the squirrel

perched, perfectly still, on the lip of the garbage bin. I

picture its soft, little lungs, flaring like a dahlia. It's true, my
mother refused to howl like the dog they called her; my father once

glowed. Inside, there is a desk, and on it, a flower head made

of paper. It says *Mom.* It has six petals around it that
unfold, a list of possible destinies—

> *You take great care of me.*
> *You cook for everyone.*
> *You hear what I have to say.*
> *You always cheer me up.*
> *You love me.*
> *You are the best.*

—and a wire stem wrapped around the frame of a faded photograph:

a man with thinning hair and jutting cheekbones, his arm around
a girl, six or seven, in a traditional yellow kebaya. The drawn

curtains behind them admit no stones. Her eyes squint, she is

smiling. Mouth small. Red, like a liar's word.

THE YEAR OF THE SHOE

A child, perhaps, one of many, sat, arms folded
at a desk painted the color of seafoam—also one
of many. The wood had not been sanded; often,
it splintered the sides of her hands as she lashed
slippery knots of alphabet around the pack of dogs
leaping from her throat. Afternoon fell in slats
upon her so that she was at once brown and yellow—
light crowded with the honking of cars, flies
and their notions of sovereignty, falling sanely
on the police who directed traffic to and from
the school, notorious for their sticks and the pigs
they shared their living rooms with. I say *perhaps*,
because it could be anyone in that country, during
that time, who had a secret, or was a secret, in that
there were many whose kidneys had not been
spilled in the fields, nor were found blue and tangled
among roots of the mangrove, nor like thunderheads,
vanished once the ditches were flooded, the streets
waist-deep in shit. Nothing was less remarkable
than that child, her waiting a pinky bone among
the rows of waiting, for an afternoon sticky
with papaya juice and tumbling into the leaves
like kites, her obedience no more than the other
obediences, which, combined, rendered a room of sixty
first-graders quieter than grass waiting for the spade.
Quiet was the price of a nation to call our own—every-
one knew this—and so she did not hear the bullets'
laughter in the spines of East Timorese girls, boys
clapped to dust in the red hands of the Santa Cruz
cemetery, no, the child's memory of that year
was of the rock she felt in her shoe minutes
before dismissal, how she tried to ignore it,
how it bit back with its single tooth, so that at last

without full consideration of the consequence, she
slipped out her foot and reached down to turn the shoe
over. A small click where rock hit the floor, and
looking up, she met the gaze of her teacher, like lava
hardening or the night that stumbled in like a drunk
through the door of the shack, where she had once
visited with Mother to see that a teacher lived much
like the police, with pigs not for eating, but for breeding
and selling to keep the lamps lit. But a teacher's words
were second only to Father's, so that day she licked
the tips of the sentence like goat-meat: *stand*
on the bad foot, in front of the classroom, for one hour.
The child watched her friends peel away, like husks
and hair from a cob of corn until the rows were
fat with their absence, guilty knee trembling
under her weight. She would hear none of the hard
whispers between Teacher and Father, who soon enough
would take her home and lay her facedown
on the sheet with the faded pink and purple flowers,
to paint pink and purple flowers of his own on the backs
of her thighs with the zinc—zinging—of his belt. For this
was what it took to survive, a secret among secrets,
while whole islands burned and the sea watched,
remembering nothing, filling shoe after shoe
piling on its floor like toothless mouths
with its own quiet and ambition, that it should
be the first and the last, the only year there ever was.

PROTÉGÉ—PART I

The street between the subway station and the church is narrow,
cars beaded along both sides like rosaries God in His hurry

to the rain's press conference had forgotten on top of the sock drawer.
Sidewalks like teeth crammed into too-small gums, hustling

each other for drops of sugar-rot, go on darkening, cracking for miles
under the row homes' stiff red lips until they are touching the glass

intestines: Center City, Philadelphia. An easier metaphor than
the dentist's office, where I was safe once among the white clay

molds and scalpel, a desk clear of debris, and spiderless walls where
shadows played the frangipani's romance against an iron twilight: my father,

who was calm then, and spotless, as he excised from mouths
the roots of injury. He had, of course, his magic tricks. Like asking

a seven-year-old what the number of Israel's tribes times itself is, and while
she tries to recall a desert she has never seen, and the sea behind it, which she has,

and how many names could be hiding in the grains of sand that bind the seen
to the unthinkable, pulling out with a flick of the wrist so quick it—the baby

tooth, like childhood itself—might not have existed at all were it not for the hole,
tasting of iron and twilight, its truth cauled now in the clearest jar of alcohol, maudlin,

almost, under the plastic Christ's painted damage, glancing off other primeval
truths, pre-cavity, boiled-egg white, never to be part of her speech again.

DISCERNMENT

Because we were

                              unwanted. We

        tied the children to the elephants of

our hearts, sent them
                    small
            swaying   to the Country of Wanting. Where

            "I"

        seem the only way to reach

            "you," not

                        "*aku*" for the friend, "*saya*"
                            for the stranger. As though

            "you"

        didn't need convincing, trick-

                        ery even, to
                        open
                        the gates one

day. The girls' faces the next

            nothing. A long white
            field like the rabid dog's tongue. On which
            neon-wreathed windows

fell like crumbs,

"I"

express pity. By putting a hand light-

ly on the throat

"you" increase

pressure when

"I"
open to the sun's brutal
           podium.   Out

                    spills shame, rice
                from a cut. What

                                        do

Americans know about. Dreaming when

our girl was little, she

                              ate chrysanthemum-peppered
                              earth not thinking about
                              women and men
                              gold buried
                              alive in chrysanthemum-scented

earth. The ragged

                    pines. She
                    tells herself fire is

    her parent. Its evacuation of
        context, thick

skin.

"I,"

mob of circumstance. Oeuvre

of plastic bags, god-
size. Headlights through
blue-tipped fingers,

the oncoming train.

ELEGY WITH A WHITE SHIRT

The way we waited for the year to end

made me think of walking backward under a mandrake
sky, cloth rough and hot with my own breath on my cheeks

as the hill began to resemble an eyelid,
the line of men in black, shields pressed side by side like a howl

spelled out, its lashes.

In the solid lake, one of the shadows had started a fire; heavy things
spilled across the asphalt. I remember thinking I

knew what violence was: verdicts left under stones

in my body and how specific
the shapes I could fold into in the cold of a wrong

train; how

electrifying, those veins appearing in the window, the city's false
sleep, lashes separating as they swept

down toward the dark mass in which I was
one strand of smoke.

༄

That was years ago, in another country,
where as a rule, people carried rain inside

them like small hammers.

In Orozco's *Combat* a blade is thrust through the suggestion of a body

inside a white shirt. I see a fist pushing
the blade in, and the blade coming clean through

the bracket where the ribs should be. There is no blood.
The shirt is holding

a line with other shirts like a wave

cresting backward against its own dark sea
pounding from the opposite shore,
suggesting an endlessness to struggle and within, fire's

vanity. From behind, I see what the white shirts cannot: faces

afloat in the umbrage of raised blades, trying to make
their way here. Maybe I am trying
to make my way there. It is not always clear

these days whether between here and there, I am supposed to break or
hold the line.

❧

In my homeland, the people wear white to signify readiness to die.

My homeland lives like a witch in my house, turning the rice
yellow and filling my mouth with marbles

when my mother calls. She puts up strange lights
in the air of my mind; sometimes they bark like dogs and when

the mask of gasoline sticks too zealously, I stop what I am doing to lick it.

Under the white shirt, the wound is longer
than any blood. Under the parade of the pure, the wind-defying
veils of redemption, my bones suggest spill.

I dig

around them day and night for the poem as irrigation; myself

as probable. Which is to say here, not there, part
of the we, not sweeping bloodless

       liquidity time and again some call bad magic and others,

America. They, everywhere, is
whomsoever we least believe. I've never seen
the witch in my house in a white shirt.
I've never seen her write. But her verdict I feel

behind every line, burning

∾

or not. For instance, mingling ashes with snow, wondering
where "my" portion of pavement begins and if today

the kids at Berks Family Detention Center are mending

their own snowpeople.
Kids whose cards to Santa have found *The Guardian*
instead, questing that old burglar—pinnacle of red in whom grows fat

our love for the obsolete like wet

       fruit in jaws of snow—*para*

la libertad. The ironclad
irony sticks in an old hole in my ribs. On white paper, neon-
colored squiggles, erratic lines suggest

stars,
flowers,
small
hands of endless sea.

Ode on Her Last Day of Work (cowritten with Lanny Liem)

EXT. HIGH-RISE APARTMENT BALCONY — DAY.

Four aunties, feasting on leftover dim sum, lounge on rainbow-striped lawn chairs while sirens rip the net of a fuming city.

> HAIR-ROLLER AUNTIE
> What do you see?

She holds up her phone for the others. On her WhatsApp screen, a fifth auntie waves, framed by the iron thighs of the Eiffel Tower.

> HOT-PINK-LIPS AUNTIE
> Tck tck. No shame.

> FAKE-LASHES AUNTIE
> Meh. Europe is boring. For me, I want
> to go to pyramids.

> HAIR-ROLLER AUNTIE
> We just bury her husband! Now she
> don't want to stay with her kids and
> grandkids when, you know.
>> (*waves at the sky*)

> FUR-COAT AUNTIE
> Oh, hush. We also didn't stay with our
> kids.
>> (*checks her phone*)
> OK, no more Wi-Fi. Do you want another
> beer?

Angry shouts and the bleating of cars with nowhere to go mushroom from the street below. Smoke like an enormous gray horse gallops across the crimson-crowned hills. The aunties clink their glasses.

                    HOT-PINK-LIPS AUNTIE
It's not our fault. If we go out right
now, they will rob us. Or maybe more
worse than that.

                    FUR-COAT AUNTIE
But maybe we will meet young handsome
guy who is alone. Look, I put my nails
on. I get my Brazil waxed!

                    FAKE-LASHES AUNTIE
Don't call your thing that. It's not
the meaning!

                    HAIR-ROLLER AUNTIE
Calm down, calm down, we all ESL here.

                    FUR-COAT AUNTIE
Hey! Brazil is also type of peanut and
inside is smooth like butter. So what I
say is not wrong. Ha ha--

The *thump-thump-thump of helicopter blades swallows
the sky. Nearby, crowbars break into bones like
windows.*

                    VOICE IN THE SKY
Remain calm. If you are not currently
in a government-approved shelter,
return to your homes and remain inside.

                    FUR-COAT AUNTIE
My husband pay no attention. At least
for the time being, I don't need to
hear he crying like baby when he sleep.

                    HOT-PINK-LIPS AUNTIE
At least he still go home. My husband
is stuck to the casino.

                    FAKE-LASHES AUNTIE
We just working, working, and working
all the time. At home is the same as in
the factory. The men is only crying and
drinking because they have nothing to
do. They think too much. Is life good
or bad? Is waste time. Good or bad, we
don't have a choice.

                    FUR-COAT AUNTIE
Did you remember what she said before
she take the plane to Paris?

                    VOICE IN THE SKY
Remain calm! Looters will be shot on
sight!

                    FUR-COAT AUNTIE
She seeing her face in movie posters--

*Gunfire. Screams like cymbals. Helicopters nosedive
toward the city's gridlock of metal and skin. Its
glass intestines shatter.*

                    HOT-PINK-LIPS AUNTIE
I'm so sad we never watching *Mamma Mia!*

                    HAIR-ROLLER AUNTIE
To start over in new country is not
for everybody. She miss become someone
important.

*The city is sepia as a ruined film roll. A cellphone
beeps.*

                    FUR-COAT AUNTIE
        Hey! Wi-Fi come back! My kid send
        WhatsApp, they arrive in the shelter!

More beeps. Their phone-lit faces flicker, candle-
like. Massive rocks punch through the atmosphere.

                    VOICE IN THE SKY
        Remain—
              (*static*)
        not cur--
              (*static*)

                    HOT-PINK-LIPS AUNTIE
        Forget it. Let's sing. She always pick
        the same song for karaoke, right?

                    HAIR-ROLLER AUNTIE
        I don't like that song at all.

                    FUR-COAT AUNTIE
        Liar. You know all the lyrics!

                    FAKE-LASHES AUNTIE
        Siri! Play Spice Girls, "Wannabe."

                    --END--

FOR MY FATHER WHO ONCE RUBBED SHOE POLISH OVER HIS BALD HEAD

She said not to say anything, because it gave you hope, which

reminds me, here is the world

you cannot enter. Though you brought us, against

the wishes of the bougainvillea, grown in clay
pots arranged like soldiers between your daughters and the wrought
iron gate on the other side of which dogs

unleashed, licked themselves to sleep. I envy
sometimes, these days, their mud-hardened coats, shaved

as I am to a worry over my shrinking Antarctic

of time. No, it's not even that. The poem I should have
written by now, I mean. What was sliding around inside you, all

those years: my painted face speaking English

as though it never knew another purpose, while you
knelt beside a creaseless bed, a man
reduced to nothing but hours. Oh, you kept

yourself busy. Cooking, cleaning, washing, sewing, tying

my mother's shoelaces on the steps of the bus. But purpose?
That is a word for everything we have not
yet found the strength to cast away. It must have been

terrifying, your child, her thin wave

through the fluorescent walls of a McDonald's, on the first shift of her
first job. You waited and waited. For me

to come back, for anyone

to say, *You are not done yet.*

And while you waited, other things happened. Eggs
spoiled. Mirrors rusted. A child

thought herself a dog, and the rain clapped. I don't,

to this day, question your version of events. When your grandson was
little, my body attacked the hair on my head. It
fell in fistfuls, until I was half-

lunar. I felt close to understanding, then, why you did

what you did. He is sixteen now, and refusing
to cut his. All night I hear him talk with no one I can see

in a world I cannot enter. He is not worrying about getting a job.

He doesn't say, *Leave me be.* Clamps
headphones over the black grass, just like I once

did, in my greasy uniform, not

recognizing you, then

not holding my laughter. Pa,

it wasn't that you hurt me. You did. It was that you tried and kept

trying to do what you thought a father should. So that
gripping the wheel
with both hands, you picked me up

that night the moon was more touchable than any country,

from my first shift at my first job, like a man who hasn't been
shedding himself in the dark. So that

right then, looking away from you, my whole world was

smooth, not a single blade survived.

SYNDROME

I am still [T H E R E. I N] that hypothalamus. [L I G H T N I N G]
stalking the bannister. Rope: [A N T I S E P T I C. G L A C I E R:]
canvas where your petals lie [D R Y I N G.] Like lips I understand,
"Don't go," is [A C R U E L T H I N G]. To ask with matches.
Behind one ear [H O W] a hand fists around a braid, trowel [I N
T H E O T H E R]. In moments of crisis [I W A S H M Y
M O U T H]. Twice daily that prayer be [L A C E D W I T H]
spearmint. On macadam [A G I R L—F L O C K J A B B I N G
T H E I R B E A K S.] Basketballs bouncing off chain permanently
accentuate. I. [O N E C R U M B O F B R E A D] communion-
thin. Like all waves we toss [O V E R T H E W A L L G O D]
being. Ever is behind [A N D] the walls. [C H A L K] in memory I
prefer it that way: [A P A S T E L E D E N O R B I T I N G] your
cranium instead of faulty eyes which [C A N ' T.] Tell monster from
buckets clanging with rain: there. I am [I N T H A T H A N G A R]
the night grass [S T R E A K E D W I T H V O M I T] on pounding
red. Of your heart though scorpion cloud rends [F O L I A G E] what
I remember. [I S D E A T H] of illumination in its cradle. Moths
falling [L I K E A V E I L O V E R Y O U , M E] inside the cool.
Rooflessness [T H A T S T A N D S O N] twisted. [E N G I N E
O F Y O U R W A I S T] I creak. With penumbra from the beginning
shard aspiring to [D Y N A M I T E.] Dawn. [T H E S T E E P L E
T H R U S T]

Such small sorrows, these. The most honest things I own
and have no use for. I go to meeting after meeting with words like
"defense" and "community," stack assurances in red lettering on the table
beside the shrimp crackers, promise to pick up the phone no matter how
cudgelblack the sky. You are not alone, I tell terrified factory workers,
terrified parents, terror itself, you are this other condition speech
has no right to enter without a warrant—the seafaring instinct

heated like a sheet of metal, recast into a bowl where rain
collects and small islands form out of the ants' drowned ambitions.
Sometimes I think the gambler with slurred speech and shaky hands, half-
asleep in the gray folding chair at the back of the sanctuary, is God
by his capacity to survive on rumor. Plainclothes. Tinted vans. Authority
is a matter of inhabiting two origins at once: *of* and *over*. I practice
words I have to believe in like rubber soles slapping concrete

in that warehouse from half a lifetime ago, men and women
folded over sewing machines, puddles of nylon, split fingernails, their salt-
touches on unflagging needles under the watch of a fluorescent army.
At home, the piano is waiting with its elegies; its mother, the black
moon under the eye, is stirring a potful of cow bones. Forget the other
eye, which did not migrate with the rest of us. Still there, chalk-dry
in the courtyard, widening every time it sights a plane's white belly.

That a potholed street in the middling borough of Collingswood, New Jersey, bears the name Atlantic, after an all-consuming body of water.

That all-consuming is Atlas's curse to bear the heavens on his shoulders.

That after the fall of the gods, half of the heavens is darkness.

That inside the car speeding down the street, I believe I am safe from being halved.

That "I" am not a white box, but a body of water.

That white is a pattern of boys who expect to live long enough to become men.

That some of these boys are whistling by on their bikes, and behind them, clear as a dream, welcome candles in the windows framed by blooms of vervain.

That "welcome" means I thought I was not afraid of the dark.

Since the jade scrubs of the cancer ward.

Since the fluorescent grid of the factory and the vista of small bones in my father's collar while I was interpreting for the twenty-something-year-old white citizen,

> *Tell your dad he can quit or I can fire him.*

Grief had already burst its cocoon; it ate him like an army of moths from the inside.

That brown men and women kept stitching jackets under the heavens of the machines.

Welcome.

That a moth is trapped in the car with me—it will die, but I do not want to practice florescence alone.

Like a first language bleeding hearts call, *speaking truth to power*.

I don't know how they don't know that power doesn't care.

That watching fires go out will become a pattern.

That fire is everywhere, and therefore, cheap.

That the hole in my foundation is all-consuming and at its bottom a frangipani tree opens its yellow hands.

That POLICE ICE is printed in yellow or white on the jacket of the night.

That the night walks freely among the ranks of the sun.

That a body of water parted once like a red skirt, then sealed over the armored horses of Egypt.

That Whitney Houston is a bone blasting

out the car windows.

That tonight, the night after, the night after that, for as long as the distance between God and a pothole, a moth's flight will spell,

They are coming for you.

BECAUSE I MISS HER,

stay with me.
Though you are an ear I've
invented from saltless air that cracks
my skin, though I leave you.
Facing you

like this, in complete
darkness, the small hairs on the back
of my neck stand up, treading
like seaweed the heft of the Pacific.
I have been reading Ross Gay's
Catalog of Unabashed Gratitude
over and over on the train
from Camden to Philly, and mornings
when the light is blue and gold over
the Ben Franklin, like waves
breaking over my head those days
I swam until I couldn't hear my mother's
warnings of the riptide and violence
in the corals, to catch a glimpse
of the dolphins at play, I thought, to be unable
to distinguish between body and sky,
beauty and fear, must be
a kind of fortune.

I have just begun to love
the little knives of which I'm made
for their portable, alien music.
Strung by their hilts in the wind,
they make a dissonance more honest than
the half-remembered melodies I play
on the piano to please my father's
shadow standing arms crossed

in the doorway. I can't explain
how it came to be that when
something I promise to care for sickens,
I move not to heal, but to cut it
away, and this makes me question if
it is time to lay the knives down,
here, on the kitchen counter
where the blue and gold light
springing through the window, leaping
off their steel, would fill my eyes,
too slow to blink, with fast
dissolving suns.

And if it is time also to turn
my face toward the source of
that light, hidden now
behind the roof of the train at rest
in the station, and the ironwork of branches
that have borne themselves through
another indifferent winter, though
I do not feel its warmth yet,
though its generosity is
abstract to a person like me who does
my duty behind walls and cannot
manage to keep even the philodendron, with
its green abundance of hearts, alive.
Forgive me,
philodendron. I have known
only how to want certain ideas of you:
lush, unselfish, obedient in
the corner of the room, the way I am
begotten of those ideas, too.

Sometimes I dream I am
running on a rainforest's sound-
proof floor through thickets of carnivorous
flowers shot through by spears
of light lean and long as my son, who,

when I awaken, is there beside me,
blowing his horn, somehow
thriving in the undergrowth while his
mother runs from one Pacific
poised like a machete against
the whole green world, to another.
Forgive me, machete, for
reminding you what you have
been, for choosing
saprophytes
limning the black soil.

Last night, the neighborhood lights
went out, and no one thought
it was worth knocking on anyone else's
door to find out what happened,
if just for the communion of it,
the brief candle of shared bafflement, which
could have, with some hyperbole,
maybe, flowered
into a carnivorous kind of laughter,
because something had been
lost to all of us that meant
something, however minor and
transient in this part of the world. I sat
right here, like a train

stopped

between destinations, or
the part of the beach that by six p.m. would be
underwater, welcoming the going-
away of definitions for my
immediate future, while
my iPhone winked at distant
lights, risking collisions, unauthorized
editions, mis- and re-
interpretations, like immigrants. That

was how I thought of my mother
shouting from the shore, as
distant light—in her
daster and the makeshift horn of
her hands. Did you know that before
a dolphin calf is born, its mother would
sing to it, so that once it
separates from her flesh, it would
know how to come back?
Each dolphin has a signature
whistle like no other, and that is what
the decades of censorship took

from us, our mothers' singular
whistlings, a way to let ourselves be
lost at sea for a while, where the lights do not
reach, because I'd know how
to call her, specifically
her, back
to me, and not
the whip of my father, or lovers
built of the bubbling inside
a mountain, or America, which
would have me dream it and nothing
else—my mother

shining like a paranoia
of nights without electricity
and love, which all these years kept
me fastened to myself,
sharpening my knives. She
would have wanted me to ask
nicely, to volunteer
my life for an idea of my life, because
she knows what it is to send
a voice out over the water and have
nothing come back. I am

both the warning, and the letting
all of it happen.

Look how the tide eats
the darkness; the train breaks
away like a chunk of coral. I am
waiting for the shout of light
like blood in the water.

Phantasm: A Body Politic

INT. APARTMENT — DAY.

A *black-haired woman stands at the end of a narrow hallway with cracked walls, her feet bare on the stained wood floor. She is facing a full-length mirror, in which she does not appear.*

>   WOMAN
>   No change.

>   VOICE ON THE PHONE
>   Are you sure?

The woman lifts her phone, switches it to selfie view. It shows the hallway stretching behind her. In the mirror, the phone seems to float. She extends her right arm and lays her palm flat on the wall. A moment later, she raps her knuckles on it. No sound.

>   WOMAN
>   I can touch things. Feel them. But you
>   can't hear anything, can you?

>   VOICE ON THE PHONE
>   I hear your voice clear as day.

>   WOMAN
>   This must be how ghosts feel. Like they
>   have to wreck something just to let
>   themselves know they're still here.

>   VOICE ON THE PHONE
>   It'll pass, love. You can still see
>   other parts of your body, right? Not
>   your face, obviously, but--

                    WOMAN
     Yes. I can see my arms, my legs. Just
     not their reflection.

               VOICE ON THE PHONE
     You should get out of the house. It's
     beautiful outside. Not a single cloud
     and the breeze smells like the ocean.

                    WOMAN
     Really? Even here?

               VOICE ON THE PHONE
     Even there, love.

                    WOMAN
     OK. I guess I'll try. Miss you.

               VOICE ON THE PHONE
     I miss you, too.

*The woman ends the call. She turns and walks down the
hallway into the kitchen. At the opposite end, it
opens to a cramped but clean kitchen. She checks the
pantry. One can of rice and beans left.*

EXT. SUBURBAN NEIGHBORHOOD — DAY.

*The roads are deserted, the sky monstrous, roiling
with clouds like melted lead. The woman walks down
the block, checking for her reflection in every
window she passes. The effort is futile. She reaches
a supermarket with letters missing from its name,
---MAN'S, and enters through the automatic doors.
There's no one inside. She wanders down a few aisles,
where most of the shelves are empty. Mariah Carey's
"Fantasy" is playing over the P.A. system.*

                    WOMAN
Hello? Is anybody here?
        (*waits*)
Where is everybody?

The P.A. crackles; "Fantasy" dies abruptly.

                VOICE ON THE P.A.
Oh, hey there, welcome. It's the last
day of the month, so we're low on most
things, but take what you need and pay
at the self-checkout, yeah?

                    WOMAN
What the hell is going on? Why haven't
I seen anyone?

                VOICE ON THE P.A.
Haha, good one.

                    WOMAN
I'm not joking!

                VOICE ON THE P.A.
Can you keep it down? I have a terrible
headache. Just follow instructions,
please, it's not like I can call
security to find you.

                    WOMAN
Wait . . . you know I'm invisible?

                VOICE ON THE P.A.
Well, duh. Who isn't? Nobody that's
gotta get their own groceries, that's
who. New normal, yeah?

The woman's knees buckle; she drops to the floor,
stunned. She starts to cry.

> VOICE ON THE P.A.
> Ah, Christ, you're one of those. I'm
> sorry, honey.

> WOMAN
> My girlfriend said, she said it'll
> pass, and I should go out because--

> VOICE ON THE P.A.
> It's a beautiful day, right?

> WOMAN
> How did you know that? And why . . .
> why did you say I was one of--one of
> what?

> VOICE ON THE P.A.
> Well, in the beginning they tested some
> experimental drugs to try and reverse
> the spread. Didn't work but one of the
> most common side effects was short-term
> memory loss. A bunch of test subjects
> went insane, which was a logistical
> nightmare as you can imagine, so they
> made a program using your loved ones'
> voices to keep you calm. We probably
> had this exact conversation last week.
> Are you the lady with the raccoon?

> WOMAN
> Why would I have a raccoon?

> VOICE ON THE P.A.
> It's a good investment if you ask me.
> Pets are the new faces of social media!

They're pretty indispensable now for
most human-to-human interactions.
Ironic, yeah? I have an iguana myself--

          WOMAN
This can't be real.

          VOICE ON THE P.A.
Look. Maybe, someday, there'll be a
cure. They keep saying soon, soon. But
honestly? I can't even remember what
I look like. It's a lot, I know, but
we all learned eventually that having
a body isn't the same thing as being
seen.

          WOMAN
I . . . I don't . . . No. I have to go.

          VOICE ON THE P.A.
Suit yourself. Don't forget what you
came for though. We're closed tomorrow.

*Mariah Carey comes back on a high note. The woman
stumbles back toward the entrance, grabbing the few
cans left on the shelves. Before she reaches the
sliding doors, she's zapped by a wall of low-voltage
electricity. The woman howls and falls back.*

          VOICE ON THE P.A.
Self-checkout only, please. Just follow
the instructions and we'll be fine--

          --END--

PASTORAL IN WHICH A DEER'S THIRST IS
THE TRAGIC HERO

Years ago, I walked just like this, from a town's one end
to the other under a church's bouquet of fire. It sang

through its steeple, of the deer's longing for the stream and mine
for something I couldn't name, something like a throat

of white silk, like the gown my mother bought me from
a bridal store hours before she gave the doctors

permission to unhook my father from the machines.
The walk I'm thinking of is not that final one

toward the worry lines of the hospital, though cars passed by
just like this, with shadows inside wrapped tightly around

their own plots, the metal and glass pretending to protect them
from the wind's agendas and the deer seeking water

on the other side of the road. I've learned through
sheer repetition to go in a specific direction without a plan

for how to survive. Now, as then, warnings in the periphery:
a rake's waxed tines by the hardware store's entrance,

a field throbbing with boy-pride and sweat, the white dashes
of a broken road. A deer put in motion by desperation defies

all these orders. Come here. Cease and desist. Do not. Pieces
of the sky fall like leaves on a dry streambed. The church

begins to hiss and fall away. Underneath, an abandoned cinema,
shiny black bones, rows of seats packed so tightly

even as a child I had to hug my knees to fit in. I wish I could tell
this story like someone who believes in anything—for instance,

that the journey ends with a room of blue ribbons.
He said, *Kneel,* and I did. My mind a white gown

caught in his antlers. From this distance, you could read it
as a sign of surrender to the plotlines authored by

poverty and dead grass. I couldn't turn away. Metal on metal,
metal on flesh, flesh in flesh. His cinematic rage, reels of it,

in the clicking brightness. When it was spent, I walked back, hiding
my wounds from the church my father had built with his hands

and placed over my head with love, with what I must believe
was love. I wish I could have named the riches I passed

on my way—the human doubts, the red in a cemetery of apples.
Kneel, he said, and pushed my head into the ashes.

The sun on my back was my audience, though I couldn't
hear it, what I felt, behind the water scrubbing cold

over my thighs. What could have been language appeared
as a gown ripped from my arms mid-bloom. My mother lying

on her side, turned toward the empty half of the bed.
You understand—I had to save the life I was ashamed to live.

Now here I am, walking with a deer's instinct for water,
one drought to the next, sorrow's repeating center

cut out of its premise, its aftermath.

1. There are right and wrong ways to put your mouth around the void in the metal.

2. The mother is a hidden compound.

3. The mother is a king, lonely and gray, whose crown of matches is alive.

4. Prepare for harrow and beauty. Their digressions.

5. A coastline, littered by boats and the dark dirt of desire, is battered by the notion of universality.

6. Blue and green, like a seam of locusts, intent that no grain of sand should escape what they cannot eat.

7. Of its own realm. Where the disc is chipped, it skips, repeating the same *please*.

8. Like a history of brokenness.

9. Holding her own hand, the king hurries past the sea.

10. A billion hind legs rubbing. This is how God is composed.

11. Past the white arches of whales, toward the garden's sanity, where someone is coming.

12. *Someone is coming* is the hook of the song. I believed it, with the strength of insects, the strength of kings.

13. The boy abandoned to sunflowers makes his horn by mutilating his bowl.

14. They are not so different from each other. Beauty and harrow. King and sunflower.

15. The universal is hard of hearing.

16. The mouth is a void (a compound of God) that makes promises, such as *I am coming*, while the mother's belly-dome, metallic, shines with questions.

17. Was I clear enough, loud enough, unmistakable, sweet enough?

18. The boy's blue lips are a digression. They bleed now, around the hole music makes.

19. Even light is suspended like a hooked fish in the hard, jeweled air.

20. Dowse your head.

21. Between the hidden and the shut doors.

I like to take my time between the station and the church,
to nod at elders on their lawn chairs by the entrances of corner stores
where everything from instant noodles to garden shears are sold
by insomniacs who in another life were doctors, radio hosts, kids
throwing rocks at tanks and each other. To run my fingertips across

the sun shattered on a chain-link fence and the laughter behind it.
I like to hear the brightness of my mother tongue like cans crushed into
pavement and the parakeet green of streets announcing themselves
like they've never carried a foreign passport. Good day, Morris, have you
noticed the Mole growing on your Broad? You might want to Pierce it.

So what if none of this is mine? Neither were the flying ants that broke
the floor's seams during rainy season. The lights would go out, and the dark
thrash with their hunger. I didn't know then what "no one" meant. I was
happy in my terror when dirt-feathered wings like the dead's
fingernails brushed my eyelids and the insides of my thighs. All those

years I heard and misunderstood their plans, seeping through slits
between the door and doorframe that separated the front of the house,
which belonged to us—God, family, the rotary phone's nuclear yellow—
from the part without a toilet, where two girls from the village—who washed,
swept, cooked, and whom I always thought of, conveniently, as immortal—

wrote letters, sometimes, to mothers who might or might not still be alive.
I'd offer to help when I felt like being a good person, and I did want to want
to be a good person with the capacity to believe that the deep-fried bulbs of ants
served the morning after a storm, with eggs and glasses of powdered milk,
really were seeds of the exotic pomegranate. That wings carpeting

the floor like tiny drafts of ill-fated words, words simply asking for
a breeze to shake the shapes out of them, might be elevated to some other
destination than the dustpan, than baskets of fire crosshatching the sky.
But I was already learning how to live with all those bodies crowding
my mouth; there was ever only light, and more light, after rain like that.

ODE WHERE MILK WAS RARE

O, what country

       aphrodisiac   even without her

   hair   their praise a pink-

thighed museum   O, unbearable roses   I sang

     to thorns in my wrists

   throwing   obdurate

       sand over my shoulder and into

   the new hollows galloped   horses made

         of sugar   O, self-discovery!

    the sand wants it

     slithering through bare

       toes   how aria

   everything I touch   with the blue-green seams

     in my head

          O,

fumbling   brocaded benevolence   brides

of the sea raised to foam   mad-

       ness on the rocks   make me anklets

make me parachute

      I'm reading the poem

    mosquitoes make   slapped dead on

      a Coca-Cola night

     drink

with me   shadows on the beach while

from the pan a snake

      pours white in iron light   O, noons

I was left

      alone

    with a shovel beyond

that line of coconut trees

CONDITIONS OF PEACE

1. Still, the cities smile. When I say buckle, I mean two exiles
whose origin is love: one to excise nightmare from the flesh
by embedding night in the flesh, red hands not hesitating those
long afternoons when sheets heavy with ash puffed their cheeks
in the yard where light lay bleating while stray cats in the roof
curled bonelessly around their disfigurements like shells in
the wrack line. The other a capacity the body, pressed, a slow-
leaking berry in the glass jaws of capital, has already forgotten.

2. Night with the force of religion: nothing was told, nothing was
hidden. The dictator understood more than the poet or prophet
the life of dew on orchids that smeared themselves shamelessly
on days of volcanic dust. Amaranth, midnight, plum. More than
enough to fret about. The aunt for whom confession meant spying
on the orphaned maid with the new priest-in-training. The uncle
who swore his Marlboro sticks were packed with grass. Man-size
bags of feathers in case the neighbors tried to burn us down again.

3. Sometimes when I am not speaking with my mother, because
the night survives in my flesh in unintended ways, which in turn
causes her pain, I think of her angular in hospital whites, the flies
like scrambled letters in bulbs dying over her head as she bowed
to hear the last requests of syphilitics whose last blisters were
exploding like the nation's censored histories. Men too guilty
to marry or made guilty by marriage whose solace now was her
silence, which like nothing else they'd ever seen, did not waver.

4. This is not memory, but something I should have remembered:
a dark figure sweeping roach husks from under the table at sunrise.
It paused as it lifted the pan over the short wall that separated yard
from dining hall—the dead insects were too smooth, their blackness
shared too much of the flatness of just-after-dusk. A closer look
(in the gap between the wall and the underside of clay tiles, smoke,

relentless, knuckling in slow motion the red-ribbed sky) revealed
an absence of eyes, wings, legs. Only paint, and threads of keratin.

5. A manicure takes about thirty minutes. In that time, I allow
myself not to wonder about the distances between my desk and
the salon, my desk and my mind, the salon and balconies of paddy
ripening, paddy and the scythe, paddy and the village, paddy and
the concept of green, green and camouflage, green and the agent
called Orange, agent and wire and the collapse of the epiglottis,
collapse and the faces on the boat, faces that repeat with slight
alterations, faces that do not, and my mind, slightness and beauty

6. in the sense of irretrievable behind the surgical mask and this
woman who makes hands beautiful to put her son through college,
her son and my son, my son and language I cannot give, language
that scythes, that paddies, that greens even the forearms of hell,
hell and what this woman is not afraid of, hell and a pair of human
hands, hands and wax and specters on the wall that war and dance,
war and dance, war and acetone and ultraviolet light, light and faces
that do not alter. Do not and God. Every God is a god of distance.

7. I go to the sea to drown. Not to die among the daily bodies,
their worries etched on by shrieking children and gulls. This is a kind
of silence. Sometimes I walk up and down the stairs in my house
a few times before bed to make sure the doors are locked. I see that
they are. I remember seeing and touching them moments ago. But each
time, I take the bolts in my hand and turn, just to feel them fail to turn
any further. I beat my son once because he stole. A mother, buckling,
keeps things in their places. *This* grassless history. *That* surviving night.

INTERLUDE

Dentures for Democracy

EXT. GRAND CANYON — DAY.

An iPad screen lies faceup on the narrow floor between cliffs. It flickers on. A man in a gray suit and a woman in a red blouse appear, sitting at a white desk. Behind them is a stage with two podiums facing each other.

> MAN IN GRAY
>
> Welcome to tonight's historic presidential candidates' debate.

> WOMAN IN RED
>
> It will be a night like we have never seen before, thanks to Dentists for Democracy.

> MAN IN GRAY
>
> That's right. Tonight, no politician will be able to tell an unfact on stage.

> WOMAN IN RED
>
> Well, they won't get away with it, at least.

A desert lizard with a pattern of orange stars along its green spine crawls across the screen, tail sweeping left to right.

> MAN IN GRAY
>
> We are just minutes away from the start of the debate, but I think we have time to check in with a DFD, don't we?

> WOMAN IN RED
>
> You bet.

The frame in the screen doubles to show a Southeast Asian man wearing thick glasses, a surgical mask, and a white coat. He is gripping a jar filled with a cloudy solution and appears to be sitting in the front row of the debate theater.

                    MAN IN GRAY
Dr. Syukur is the founder of Dentists
for Democracy. Thank you, Doctor, for
joining us on this very special night.

                    DR. SYUKUR
It is my pleasure. I believe we have
found at least one solution to the
crisis of faith and accountability in
our democracy, and we are of course,
honored to contribute any way we can.

                    WOMAN IN RED
Can you tell us a little bit about DFD?

                    DR. SYUKUR
Sure. We were founded after the last
election, which, as you are all aware,
was plagued by lies and incoherence;
a pandemic that became a tragedy of
unprecedented scale in this country;
and the near destruction of all our
democratic institutions, because of
the failure of our more clear-headed
leaders, despite their best intentions,
to hold the extremely powerful
accountable.

                    MAN IN GRAY
Why do you think dentists are the right
people to help our society course-
correct, Doctor?

                    DR. SYUKUR
Well, as dentists our job is to
preserve teeth and gum health. This
means, at best, preventing the
occurrence of rot and, at worst,
keeping it from spreading, including
cutting it out as needed.

                    MAN IN GRAY
Excellent, excellent. So is this what
you will be doing tonight? Cleaning the
rot?

                    DR. SYUKUR
From the mouths that are campaigning
to speak for the whole country? Yes,
absolutely.

                    WOMAN IN RED
Don't you have a preferred candidate?
Won't it be hard to maintain
impartiality?

                    DR. SYUKUR
Well, if I may speak candidly, one
does not get this close to the zenith
of global domination without some
predatory instinct. My preference
doesn't change that. Whoever it is has
to be able to handle either the pain of
losing a tooth or telling the truth.
          (chuckles)
The mouth is a bidirectional funnel,
you see. Our political leaders have
to answer for whatever it is they are
asking us, the public, to ingest.

Trumpets swell heroically from behind Dr. Syukur.
Cheers erupt like bees from a broken hive. A vulture
taps its anxious beak on Dr. Syukur's pixelated cheek.

> WOMAN IN RED
> Oh, it's starting! OK, we have to
> wrap up here, Doctor. Can you tell us
> quickly what's in the jar?

Close up, china-like bits are visible, floating in the
milky substance.

> DR. SYUKUR
> Our team, Dentists for Democracy, is
> collaborating with journalists who
> will fact-check statements by the
> candidates in real time tonight. This
> jar contains teeth from the final round
> of the primary debates. Only one party
> participated then, but thanks to public
> pressure, both are doing it now.

> MAN IN GRAY
> So when a candidate is caught making a
> false statement?

> DR. SYUKUR
> One of my colleagues will extract a
> tooth from their mouth.

> WOMAN IN RED
> Without anesthetics?

> DR. SYUKUR
> They can opt in for anesthesia but it
> would probably affect their ability to
> participate cogently in the debate.

                    WOMAN IN RED
Wouldn't the pain also affect their
performance?

                    DR. SYUKUR
Only if they lie. The whole point is
deterrence, though as you can see—
          (*holds up the jar*)
But anyway, that's the motto of the
American Dream, right? No pain, no
gain?

*The vulture barks. The cliffs exhale, sending waves
of glittering dust across the faces of Man in Gray,
Woman in Red, Dr. Syukur. Within seconds, the screen
is buried under a blanket of sand. Only a pulse
of underwater light remains, the patter of fading
applause.*

                    --END--

with a belly full of sausage, it's hard not to give thanks
for contradiction. I mean, this is not my Thunderbird,
I didn't pay for this perspiring cup of sweet iced coffee,
I have no sway over the grayness of October infecting
the miles of visible world it contains. But I do appreciate
speed, and somehow, whipping past cows in their somber
contemplation of the wet earth, their tails swatting at flies,
which I guess could be the bovine manifestation of social
anxiety, makes me feel like a body beyond history's gambit.
We pass so many lumpy fields yet to be gleaned (meaning
my eyes could have bled from the monotony) and pastel-
colored homes spaced so far apart I can't help thinking, no
wonder folks in these parts voted for the orange psychopath
obsessed with building a wall, but for the most part, keep
our promise to act like this is one big adventure, a hurtling
away from, not toward, the consequences of powerlessness.
I'm in the passenger seat and Henry, whose nephew will
be facing the judge today, is punching the pedal like a god-
damn Doctor Who while taking strategic bites of his croissant
so as not to get buttery flakes all over the red leather seat.
In between, he regales me with his early years in America
(he was a banker back home) scrubbing toilets in exchange
for a sushi chef apprenticeship. (He's a restaurateur now).
I, too, offer tales of sacrifice and survival, because well,
what else do you do while you are being hunted? The rain
paints its fleeting destinies on the car windows, and I think
of the common itineraries adventure takes: escape from
point A to point B, or, return, i.e., anywhere you go ends up
point A. There was one night, a long time ago, in a car
like this one but stolen, in another country, with the top
down, when I beat my chest at the moon because I couldn't
scream with all that wind, a whole country of wind,
rushing down my throat. I was a runaway then, a dropout,

a fuckup, and still I get nostalgic about the colors of those
days, lead and mulberry, how one chased the other, lightning
in my periphery when I threw my fists at the boys and the law.
They landed nowhere, and I'm not even mad, because escape
is the story we tell so we can live with the echoes of choices
we made in greed, hunger, pain. Right now, Henry is saying
that his daughters have no time for him, so, *I will treat you
like you are one of them.* This isn't the first time I've been
a stand-in; it could be the closest thing we've invented to time
travel. He's standing in too, for my dad, who would have never
driven a Thunderbird (he was the kind of guy who hit the brakes
every few seconds when there was no other car on the road. Plus
he was a dentist.), or stopped at a gas station just to let me buy
a pack of cigarettes. At some point, I stop trying to find aesthetic
value in the cows' sad, lolling heads. Ahead of us the prison,
with its crown of barbed wire, rises out of the dead grasses
like solid blocks of rotten milk. I've never been here, but I almost
cry with recognition. Of course. Of course. There is where I've
left my heart, in the box of metallic things you can't bring inside.
Henry parks his beautiful machine and we walk toward the blue
doors, naked without our gadgets, not touching but leaning toward
each other—he's my dad's height, shorter than me—in the dogged rain.

THE ROOTS DO A LIVE COVER OF
MAYFIELD'S "MOVE ON UP"

Bilal cries **DEAR GOD** and Black Thought

STROKES

entendres in his beard. **A SHADOW** splits

THROAT

the light confetti with a brass

WRAPPED around his waist. What

is the tipping point   after which nothing

LOST once, twice can be

lost again?

Once, I

WALKED

up the driveway to find

MY FATHER smashing

The Roots Come Alive and

The Rose That **GREW FROM CONCRETE**

with a broomstick.

Dear **INDIGO GRAMMAR**. Dear never-to-come-home-again hanging on for the by-and-by. **IN**

this **CHARYBDIS** of

GOLD-STUDDED

angers, sweet as peaches
soaking the weft of their own
plucked selves. I'm

SO FAR FROM the last bed you
slept in. Nobody

gets a better view. Tonight

I'm

LUCIFER falling   toward a hip human perfection.
Call it

I LOVE YOU, TOO, Pa.

This song, even

A DAMAGED GOOD

KNOWS ALL THE WORDS

Back on the island, Ganesh lived, crouching, just outside my parents' bedroom window. At dusk, I often caught him staring at the scepters of papaya and orchid our neighbors laid at his feet. That they'd spoil untouched on the dishes woven of banana leaf was an object lesson in contrast and comparison: my parents' I Am That I Am, once mad for the scent of burning animals, had evolved to desire no more than our most private language about our most banal humiliations. For years I heard His voice, felt it at my back like the crisp white of bougainvillea spilling through the gate's metal bars. In stadiums where we were packed by the tens of thousands, I saw it fell grown men like timber and reassemble them for maximum yield in the free-market economy. Oil. Tourism. Slums and slush funds for the Smiling General. Two countries later, I still hide my jealousies. Like the uncle who would not bend, who gambled even the steel braces of his house and left his children with nothing but the imprint of a cross in a gray palm. It had to be enough.

Listen.

There was a head of hardened lava, a lantern in the mountains. A god built from the opened graves and over him, the night hung like a hammer.

ZUIHITSU WITH LOVE FOR THE MOON'S FAILED REBELLION

You showed me a long, winding road that cut through a tapestry of frost. The refinery's

rust-armored cylinders rising from massive, defeated grass. Smoke had stopped

writing letters and the workers with oil in their ears are now elsewhere, illusory, bouncing grandbabies on arthritic knees. Florida,

probably. I put my lipstick on before I looked

for the world. That room made of moon and metal guesses. The desk rain abandoned. Like your hand, Klingons are approaching

the home planet, resolved to defend their heat to no one. *We do not have the luxury of principles*, says Starfleet Admiral Cornwell. My principles

crept

        horizontally as frost would. I wanted to leave

the world racing with flies, a cord over the normal river, where one brother would squat to take a shit ten feet down from the other scrubbing his arm-

pits with ash. *That is all we have*, says Starfleet mutineer Michael Burnham, because she knows even

in *Black Panther*, it is nobility that wins the day. Who wouldn't gladly

trade the frosty ballot box for a damp room with a beaded curtain and a ten-dollar massage at any time of day on any corner of Denpasar's streets. Effortless, unlike the striving

husband who drops her off by the lilied entrance because he doesn't think
women should drive.

She steps out of her clothes in air black as a lily. Lies

face down, and within minutes, consciousness is a question of pressure.
Where, how deep, how

close to bleed. *If you speak it means you remember*, writes Kimiko Hahn. After
the footage ended, the refinery was pressurized

tundra. I am not a democracy. Or my mother in her intact stratosphere. My
childhood friends,

long and moneyed, debate whether to cut one more fold or stab—to better
shade the moon—another row of lashes, one by one, into the skin of their
eyelids. The villa did not ask for

air conditioning because it had no walls. Prime altitude. Voices like tigers

crouched behind mahogany beams. I wept like a staircase, widening at
the bottom for purely aesthetic reasons. The lipstick was already on you. I
marked you, THE WORLD, without

 your consent. Morgana. Callisto. Koba. Killmonger. Are you

there. I reserve my love. For the antagonists whose pain is moonlight spilled
on the dead factories. The speaker is linked to the writer by a tenuous string
of spit. She hums

like a microwave, walking toward that pool of moon, where her father stands,
the mouth in his face aglow. Her government, ready

for the rebellion to turn on itself. Accusation that looks like SLUT, but

the moon bottles it up. *I choose and cherish / all that will perish*, argues June
Jordan. *The living deal.* From which there is no coming back. In Singapore,

several aisles in a single drugstore are dedicated wholly to skin-bleaching products. The father suspects something. His wife has sold too many shoes. She keeps the most coveted pair—ivory—for herself. As is her way. She can't even wear them, so broken is the skin of her soles

from years of walking barefoot on dung and crushed

brick on the way to and back from the market, defending her mother's

little plastic bags of homemade soy sauce. In a rare season of certainty, I used the last of

my credit to visit an exploded planet. Pressure of Achillean magnitude pulverized debris to the fineness of an eyelash. *My normal life*

ended the second my parents put me on that ship, says Supergirl to a wide-eyed Jimmy Olsen after punching the carburetor right out of a car. Normal is losing, then

losing some more. Your hand is being filled with the Holy Spirit, having

what others desire and you can't escape. My mother carries her secret, useless

shoes everywhere. *Why do you eat so fast*, she chides. *Like the devil is right behind you.* The sun a leather

black rose over

the slapping of knife on bread in the kitchen. My lipstick set to announce its last will and testament. On the Lunar New Year your hand weighs, I have no idea what. I wanted

to say, *Yes, I'll float with you, I'll love*

the short-circuiting under your suit, the lying design, but couldn't break out of the moon

my father fermented. Nearing climax, a door scorched like a word that
remembers nothing. It is

snowing in my eyelashes. Which is to say, forgive me. I was born

> a hammer tapping on a lock. The hammer did not
> hope to open it. It just wanted to hear a song—any
> song's—primal, inexplicable

> evil. *They made*

a machine to make climate change happen where white people don't live, says my
Lyft driver.

And I'm puertorriqueño. Don't. My knee is

a child filled with worms. It would seem

the noblest of us have made of throne a mercy. Yielding to the rust-hearted,
mongers and mongrels, not arms but panoramas of the believable world
never

to be seen again. Beneath acres of frost, how moonlight—

AFTER THE FUNERAL

A train of wax paper draped over wobbly-footed tables, the red
perfectly matching the towering golden Buddha's

loincloth. Lips flap. Planets
wound around chopsticks unravel, drip

bits of scallion. Our fists fill with bulbs of cheap
porcelain. After love: the patient parse of meat

from bone. Yolk from destiny. Kin do not
recognize each other

in this steaming nation. A mint leaf on my tongue
makes me forget my tongue. Several

languages eddy, their thorns snagging through
rain's arrhythmia. Misunderstanding, our common feast.

Auntie who runs circles around
the Hells Angels this side of town with her migrant

English and smudged mascara jumps up after spilling
bright orange Fanta on her leather miniskirt.

Uncle who can quote any passage from
Corinthians on command waves his napkin

at her moon-thigh: *I surrender! I surrender!*
Roses of Sriracha. The whale of sad laughter rocks

us on its salty back. It saves
us, this indecency. Beyond the glass

storefront, gray sonata of city, the juniper's
judgment tearing at elbows. A boy with

a dead man's name is stitching himself inside
a just married teenage girl. She is

laughing too, as though she could still
belong to anyone. The sun

had rendered every pebble and worm like a confession
on the opened ground. It cowers now

while our oil-slick teeth grow winter-big. Have they
forgotten? Have I? To unbutton the hawk

from the white and black keys of the piano. To rewrite
everything.

Ancestral Agendas

EXT. ROOFTOP - NIGHT.

*In the heart of a ruined downtown, a square brick
building rises, intact. Each corner of its rooftop
is adorned with a neon sign leaning on rusty beams:
"Drink Now Die Later"; a pair of ox horns; the blue
cross of the Church of Jesus is Refuge(e); and a
lightbox announcing, "Dawn of the Queer Dead 7:45."*

> VOICE OF ANCESTOR ONE
> I can't believe this is finally
> happening, I've been waiting for . . .
> well, I'm not sure actually, who keeps
> track after they're dead, eh?

> VOICE OF ANCESTOR TWO
> I don't think he's ready.

*The access door creaks open and a lanky, brown teen
emerges, carrying an instrument case.*

> VOICE OF ANCESTOR ONE
> Why would you say that? We've been
> cultivating this one for . . . well,
> again, I'm not sure, but they're
> definitely bigger now, aren't they?

> VOICE OF ANCESTOR TWO
> I'm just saying. There are a lot of
> distractions. Hurricanes, earthquakes,
> fires, pandemics, white supremacists--

> VOICE OF ANCESTOR ONE
> All those things were around when we
> were--

                    VOICE OF ANCESTOR TWO
          --YouTube, Twitch, Instagram, Tiktok,
          whatever that shitshow is they're still
          calling the news, protests--

                    VOICE OF ANCESTOR ONE
          OK, boomer.

The teen unzips their hoodie, peels off their
oversized jeans. A silk white gown blossoms from the
stalk of them.

                    VOICE OF ANCESTOR ONE
          Gorgeous! Absolutely gorgeous!

                    TEEN
          It's my mom's old wedding dress.

                    VOICE OF ANCESTOR ONE
          Oh! Shit. You can hear us?

                    TEEN
          Um, yeah. You guys are like the worst
          whisperers ever.

                    VOICE OF ANCESTOR TWO
          Hm. That's unusual. Maybe not even
          legal. We should check with--

                    TEEN
          Take a chill pill, ok?

The teen unlocks the latch of the instrument case.
From its dark folds, they take out a silver mouthpiece
and a polishing cloth.

                    VOICE OF ANCESTOR TWO
Do you think you've practiced enough? I
just noticed you were spending a lot of
time on Twitch specifically, and--

                    VOICE OF ANCESTOR ONE
Can you stop being so negative please?
Our job is to promote positivity--

                    VOICE OF ANCESTOR TWO
Yes, and before, our job was to avenge
and punish, but times change, and
the ancestor market wants something
different, so. Kid. Listen. A lot is
riding on your performance tonight.
Cosmically, I mean. Do you understand?

The teen squats to affix the mouthpiece, now gleaming
like a tiny dolphin, to a dull-coated, scarred French
horn.

                    TEEN
Not really. Why do I have to redeem you
guys? You're supernatural beings, why
can't you do it yourselves?

                    VOICE OF ANCESTOR TWO
We're nobodies, kid. Literally, now.
This one was a petty bureaucrat who
took bribes--

                    VOICE OF ANCESTOR ONE
Hey, we were barely paid, OK, I had to
feed my family.

                    VOICE OF ANCESTOR TWO
You turned a blind eye when the
imperialists ransacked--

                    VOICE OF ANCESTOR ONE
You were a pirate! How many people did
you personally kill and rob?

                    VOICE OF ANCESTOR TWO
I had no choice! My whole village was
burnt to the--

                    VOICE OF ANCESTOR ONE
Whatever.

                    VOICE OF ANCESTOR TWO
          (*sighs heavily*)
We were people with limited options.
And now we're cogs in the afterlife
machine. Our frustrated dreams have to
come true before we can retire.

               TEEN
And your dream is for me to play
Tchaikovsky's Fifth Symphony to an
abandoned city?

                    VOICE OF ANCESTOR ONE
Well, my dream was for my daughter to
marry a rich European and improve our
family's fortune. But then, she died.

                    VOICE OF ANCESTOR TWO
I wanted to see an opera live at the
Bolshoi Theatre.

               TEEN
          (*gestures at themself*)
So this is a compromise.

VOICE OF ANCESTOR ONE

Well, yes, but after this, you're free!
You can do anything you want. Believe
in yourself! Follow your heart!

TEEN

I don't know what I want. Preparing for
this took all my time and energy.

VOICE OF ANCESTOR ONE

Oh.
     (laughs nervously)
Well, you'll figure it out!

The teen is quiet for a long while. Then they reach
into the bell of the horn and pull out a pale, yellow
tulip. They tuck it behind their ear and turn to walk
away.

VOICE OF ANCESTOR TWO

Hey! Where are you going?

TEEN

I'm out. I don't owe you anything.

VOICE OF ANCESTOR ONE

No, you can't . . . You can't! Please!

TEEN

Keep the horn. It'll be good company
for you guys. You're basically wind,
right?

--END--

YOU DON'T HAVE TO BE TOUGH ALL BY YOURSELF,
YOU SAID

and if I returned the favor, it was much later. Or
I lied. At the airport, waiting for my turn to sleep. Like a leg
bone inside a grasshopper. In the selfie I sent, darkness

curtains one side of my head which hasn't thought
of Christopher for years. Aside from his occasional Facebook
posts captioned #blessed below boys in blue

jerseys despite the Canucks' losing streak. The Rockies
look Photoshopped, but not the beetle-like sacs
under his mother's eyes. All seasons, petals by a Jacuzzi. Cherry-

flavored hospital Jell-os on the lid of the grill. Unless
they're margaritas, O, winking emoji #FUCKCANCERGOCHEMO!
I should've sent his mother a letter. Something about that year

everyone could see what was hidden under the oversized
T-shirts, and Chris carried my books between History, Biology,
Advanced Lit. Plotted with Mr. F to find me among Mrs. F's

old maternity clothes something to wear for the prom. How
rotten the colors on those dresses. In open air the moth
holes like tiny kisses that year I wanted to

leave my life lipstick on the road. Chris-of-the-roses-in-his-chest
saying, *You will be*

                    a great mom. Where

is the ocean where the faces of glaciers fall apart. I wrote
a poem instead about the woman with red glasses who after a
Know-Your-Rights training gave me her Notice to

Appear stamped Department of Homeland Security. Nobody
wants to go home, Chris. Nobody wants their theory of the earth
proven. Because I did not believe in kindness, I did not have to see

       it. All day

I feel my love tug at me from the other side of a blue clarity.
I text him my face when I think it most
untouchable. WAKE UP. The marshaller is waving

her orange batons. Most days, a pilot
reads the signs and nobody dies.

RECURRING

The ocean pulls, is pulled,
                    pulling back like a bedcover, but

instead of drape, rears
            up on legs   foam-

                    flower legs, banished
            from the light legs with the deep

wide, scars of rock and glue.
                    Crushed,

                            crushing, crushes bone. Covers

the sky, the blue-
                    black with the blacker drugged
                            dance of whales crossing out

the staring starred   harpoon tips.
                            Mountains, cliffs
                                    drum up stampede

                                    legs, bulbous, boiling

the patience-less legs, water has
            a velocity angering, god's debasement

                    hovers. Ran-after

moon
            bounces off the smooth lid
            father's head, like a bottle's

shiny, shined, lying simile   because he hated, is hated,
alcohol.

                                   Breathless run,
wrung, mother,
                         sister already out of site,

bright fire   barking eyed,   eyeful of the forest of dogs

have been loosened, lure
             of the delinking muscles.   A blinkered

moon into
a mouth

the size of a basement,   a bulb with a waving, waived

                   legs. Follow. Breath heat

in ocean endangered
air, airing

                              armed teeth. Arms, white as the whetting
roof,   looks

                         up brief, flanks of god's
                         beef, our cysts of fat,

                                   fragility. Will remember

the floor ended,

               is an ending quickly, then mouth
                         through mouth,
                                  the chasm and rope like tooth

edge over it, end
          to end. The crater   of father has been
                         stepped

          steeping black
polished foot after foot   on the fraying, frays woven of arms

                knifed out, offering the self's offing

      cheap metal while flames

      finger, filigreed. Greedy   the dearness of this loved

              with ocean
poised, poisons   the missing we had been left,
              leaving,
        behind this heaving
              mouth with the leaves
                  made of dogs on the other

side. I make, am made

voice veering from the mouthed, mutinous
        tin dying on tongue   volcanic while he halo.
            Goo and grammar.

Father grass.   Father vertigo.   Father long without

        doesn't look back
            at his love, at loving
                  in the ream of mine
        flooded by moonlessness
            to Möbius.

He was
isn't
will reach,

        reasoned by flames
          licking, whose villain
        language on the rope

that his is going home.

It husks me.

It does how
to resolve, this

hole I hold like hellish

velocity. Stopped as just is when, felled.

My father's signature began with a bold O, the ink looping
at its top before scrawling illegibly away: from right to left it looked
like a worm wriggling its way into a mouth rounded by wonder.

I practiced forging it as much for the pleasure as necessity—it didn't
fit the way he crossed his arms while surveying the white tiles for fugitive
strands of hair, or how I paid for every dirt stain on my hand-me-down

jeans with a berating. It was his claim to love Elizabeth Taylor though
his head would nod into his chest halfway through any one of her films;
the sound of petals drying redly on his canvas, which reigned over

the dining room while volcanic ashes like manna rained. O, dandruff
of heaven! Give us this day our daily transfixion, who are built of primary
colors and childlike palms waving to every tourist for their magnificent

scraps! He dreamed of windmills, the absence of dog shit in rivers
we praised as a symbol of God's deliverance. One winter, he drove me
and my sister to a Christmas tree plantation near the city limits

in Richmond, British Columbia, where a scarlet windmill stood
like a man struck by sudden, perfect understanding. Night was filing into
gaps in the rows of fir like a reserve battalion, or memory, mixing

with the patches of frozen mud where trunks in their green gowns,
now being lashed onto the roofs of station wagons, had kept the snow from
collecting, while false bells and true laughter chimed, and the moon,

our one faith, rolled back its eye. My father pointed at the enormous,
frost-hushed blades above us and said, *That is why we came*. I could not
forgive him for that, not while he lived, not when they thawed under

spring's eagerness and still did not stir. He's somewhere else now like snow emptied of the axe's ringing, while I lose sleep over my forgeries: this hand, this eyelid, this piece-by-piece abandonment of a plan of escape.

IN EUROPE, MY MOTHER WEARS SHADES

so I can't see her eyes when I'm taking her picture
by the Prinsengracht canal, in the breeze of
the evergreen windmill in Zaandam churning out
brightnesses for centuries-dead Rembrandt with a deck
overlooking farmlands so vast and flat I almost
mistake them for inevitability; under titanic
walls of three different cathedrals all named for a single
man, Bavo, the no-good soldier who got himself
sainted for redistributing wealth he married into, then
one for an emperor whose posthumous application
for sainthood was not approved by the pope and who had
instead a golden bust made, into which later, his skull
was deposited so that it could be carried ahead of his
successors, on the day of their succession, on a carpet I
imagine is red, as an emblem of his presence or rather, his
continuing, authorizing principle for those who
would kill or let die, save or let live, the citizens
or not, of empire. My mother decides she too, will

walk through the white heat of Europe inside
a kind of bust: shawl, hat, sunglasses like black moons
floating on her face, which makes me think of the surface
of water, tamed, no longer subject to tides, which is
everywhere here. You can't miss the whooping men, women
in bikinis goldening their bodies amid a firework of water
on a plain Thursday afternoon—water that from the bridge
the boat engines seem to gash, the gashes strewn
bits of lace, before the skin shuts again, brown and in-
scrutable. My mother *tck tck*s my newly adopted
habit of standing in narrow lanes in front of windows with
curtains drawn aside to mentally catalogue types of furniture,
books, how a woman slips on a blue dress and considers
her shoulder bones in the mirror, the dog napping, a father

slitting grilled fish for two small children, who stare back
frowning, perhaps a little afraid of the tan, black-haired woman

blocking the sun's pilgrimage into their kitchen.
Once, we were forced off the barely existing sidewalk
by a plastic gate around a woman and her baby who were
sprawled on the street curb just outside a dim, narrow
house (lime-green sofa, white walls, rattan barstools by a long
white countertop, low bookshelf doubling as a table). More
than once, there are men, young and muscled, quite beautiful
really, very Joel Kinnaman—maybe they're all related, these guys, if
not by blood, then by money, if not money, then a secret boot
camp for beatific men or some other clandestine inheritance—
lounging in briefs among deliciously disheveled sheets,
one hand around the neck of a beer bottle, while the other
hovers over a screen, where I imagine they are tracking
stocks like soft rabbits or whatever it is rich, sculpted men
do on hot summer afternoons with the French doors thrown open
to an envious world, and I do mean beautiful, in the sense
that even statues of once-living soldiers stationed to
stand on the ledge of a castle tower to watch the night, which

must have been so much more invincible then with nothing
but stars in it, have also been cast in gold, beside kings
on horseback and swans and angels and disciples of Christ in a
desperate front against tarnish—replaceable men, who, if they
slept on the job, would have plummeted headfirst
to the cobblestones below where dogs without masters
clicked their paws and tourists now toil with hidden, cloudy
hearts, that weird longing to disappear from the middle of our own
lives, where it is impossible to distinguish history from
the way a tomato reflects back fluorescence on its taut skin, is
caressed, then chopped . . . perhaps I just miss the tomato's
alien being. . . . I am not immune. In Charlemagne's cathedral
in Aachen, I run my fingers over blue-veined marbles,
marveling at their cool confidence (in an earlier draft, I wrote
stoicism, but "stoic" implies a certain performativity in the face of
adversity that is absent from these surfaces which seem, rather,

fulfilled in their severe geometries) and of course we
learn of the repairs—revisions, really, given how much has been
added, how much taken away—tiles, chandeliers, stained
glass but especially scenes along the wall
circling the apse, where centuries have rubbed away
arms, legs, faces, torsos from the most recently painted
(Byzantine, because I *was* listening to the tour guide) version
of the holy community. It's almost a joy. What they
call unrecoverable, I call almost gone. My mother
drops a euro into a metal pot and takes off her shades before
lighting a single candle to stand for her daughters, grandson, sons-
in-law, and last living sister. Maybe that's all God is.
The idea of taking something off, scrubbing away a layer,
until all you have is the dark egg of a woman's
face, a plane of light unblemished by her life's details.
Then on the train, the pastoral passing-by of strong-kneed
cows with brown, white, and spotted coats, the blue gaze
of empty swimming pools and freshly painted steel
beams in every station, a fort on a hill from whose burnt

battlements the moon rises. My mother tells me
things about our family, about love and grief being part of
a long-term strategy, choices made about whom, when,
and how to lose just enough but not too much, a math
I will not reveal to you, reader, though it might
clarify certain angers, might suggest or amplify the resonance
of particular images that could enrich your experience
of this poem as a flotation device . . . because here's
the thing. I am my mother's daughter. A woman who
crossed the Pacific Ocean without relatives or friends to
greet her or a language she could speak on the other side.
At dusk, the tourists lean back and swing their legs
along the banks of the canal. I am staring into windows,
casting my brief, slightly malevolent shadow on the family
sitting down to dinner. Sorry for what? My mother would never
let you see her watching at all.

Indigo. Amaranth. Magenta. Willow. Dusk. You have to choose. When to layer, where to darken. You want the angle of the light, the direction of its falling, to be consistent. This is how you give depth to a figure that has only warmth and a finite amount of time. This is how you make them believe you: his hands, kneading the dough for the bread-maker we will use every week for one year exactly. His snoring with the dog-eared recertification exam book yellowing on his lap while the rain picks off needles from the evergreen. The way rose hasn't left the rims of our eyes since we arrived. He doesn't give up talking to God. At some point I think he must begin to suspect it's a one-way conversation, though he still insists that a choice not aligned with God's will is a mistake. In other words, a choice is not a choice or it is something you have to pay for. At least the performance of a conversation is free. God is a poem to recite over and over when what one feels, what one desires, eviscerates in the morning air. He kneels on the freshly vacuumed balding carpet in a freezing room with emerald windowpanes, holding our hands, saying, *Father*. The bus she rides to the mountains is cobalt; then, for twelve hours she horseshoes her spine over a silver desk, one of hundreds of women who have shed their tribes, families, languages, their old weapons, to cross the ocean, to be counted among the fluorescent angels of capitalism. On her way home, an asteroid splashes on the face of the earth. Believe it or not, this happens every day. You have every color before you and the margins of every page in your school notebook asking for a more radiant life. He won't go to bed until you are done, because you might make a mistake; the coloring pencils, oil-based, the only things in the apartment not purchased from a thrift store or a garage sale, are non-erasable. Of course, he cannot help you. You are not a poet. You are making a wolf. You are making a hatchet.

ILLUSTRATIONS

All photographs courtesy of Cynthia Dewi Oka.

Page 21

2019. An abandoned plane on a hill in the middle of land set aside for development in Negara, Bali.

Page 42

1985. After a lifetime of hard labor and several miscarriages, a Chinese Indonesian woman cradles her firstborn on the porch of her rented house in Denpasar, Bali. Her husband inspects teeth for a living. She is wearing her best shoes.

Page 60

1975–80. He was not always a father. I try to remember that. Once, he set his jaw at something directly ahead that no one else could see, and there was no surrender in him.

Page 80

1992. The girl she used to be is a woman's first ancestor. This one plays the piano, the tips of her feet like stray puppies nosing their reflections on the floor, mistaking it for meat, for herself.

Page 93

2013. The house, rotted by years of neglect after the family left. Like memory, it stands over us. The sky falls through its holes.

ACKNOWLEDGMENTS

With thanks to the editors of the following publications, where some of these poems first appeared, sometimes in earlier versions:

Academy of American Poets: "Redacted from a Know-Your-Rights Training Agenda—" and "The Roots Do a Live Cover of Mayfield's 'Move On Up'"
Court Green: "Art of Revision"
Hot Metal Bridge: "Syndrome"
Hyperallergic: "Pastoral in Which a Deer's Thirst Is the Tragic Hero"
Kenyon Review: "Elegy with a White Shirt"
LEON Literary Review: "For My Father Who Once Rubbed Shoe Polish over His Bald Head"
Pacific Review: "The Year of the Shoe"
PRISM International: "After the Funeral" and "In Europe, My Mother Wears Shades"
wildness: "Recurring"
Scoundrel Time: "Protégé" (as a single five-part poem), "You Don't Have to Be Tough All by Yourself, You Said," and "Zuihitsu with Love for the Moon's Failed Rebellion"
They Rise Like a Wave: An Anthology of Asian American Women Poets: "Conditions of Peace"
Tupelo Quarterly: "21 Lessons in the Art of Embouchure" and "Meditation on the Worth of Anything," with special thanks to Hoa Nguyen for selecting the latter as a winner of the Tupelo Quarterly 2019 Poetry Prize
What Saves Us: Poems of Outrage and Empathy in the Age of Trump: "Driving to York Prison in a Thunderbird"
Women of Resistance: Poems for a New Feminism: "Elegy with a White Shirt"

Boundless gratitude to everyone who has encouraged me and who has made time to read, critique, listen to, and believe in these poems.

I am indebted to family, friends, mentors, and colleagues who have helped me grow into the poet these poems needed: Hari Alluri, Kaveh Akbar, Cindy Arrieu-King, Mahogany Browne, Gabrielle Calvocoressi, Franny Choi, Josh

Estanislao Lopez, Daisy Fried, Aracelis Girmay, Alexis Pauline Gumbs, Ellen Hagan, Joy Harjo, Perry Janes, Parneshia Jones, Rodney Jones, Sally Keith, Airea D. Matthews, Innosanto Nagara, Hieu Minh Nguyen, Gregory Pardlo, Laura Pegram, Willie Perdomo, Seema Reza, Patrick Rosal, Raquel Salas Rivera, Idrissa Simmonds, Vincent Toro, Connie Voisine, Jenisha Watts, Eleanor Wilner, Yolanda Wisher, and Jenny Zhang.

The writing of this book was supported by the Leeway Transformation Award as well as the Holden Minority Scholarship from Friends of Writers and the MFA Program for Writers at Warren Wilson College. A huge thanks to Debra Allbery for the literary home I needed to get out of my own way.

To Val, thank you for teaching me to live with both eyes open and reminding me that I am worth fighting for.

To my Pejuang family—Katherine Antarikso, Sinta Penyami, Regina Valensia, Aldo Siahaan, and Kristen Utomo, homeland is where you are.

To Gladys, thank you for being my better half.

To Mama, thank you for cowriting "Ode on Her Last Day of Work" with me and teaching me the English that kept a roof over our heads, that fed and clothed us. Your English is my hero.

To Sevé, my best friend, thank you for all the ways you have listened, loved, labored, and grown with me.

To Paul, you are the only country I need. Thank you for choosing me.